PROVERBS
FOR YOUNG PEOPLE

Written and illustrated by

Jack E. Levin

With a preface by his son Mark R. Levin

ALADDIN
NEW YORK   LONDON   TORONTO   SYDNEY   NEW DELHI

For the love of my life,
my beautiful wife and best friend, Norma.

For my dear children, grandchildren,
and great-granddaughter.

For children and families everywhere.

~ J. E. L.

ALADDIN

An imprint of Simon & Schuster Children's Publishing Division

1230 Avenue of the Americas, New York, New York 10020

First Aladdin hardcover edition November 2015

Copyright © 2015 by Jack E. Levin

Preface copyright © 2015 by Mark R. Levin

Jacket illustration copyright © 2015 by Jack E. Levin

All rights reserved, including the right of reproduction in whole or in part in any form.

ALADDIN is a trademark of Simon & Schuster, Inc., and related

logo is a registered trademark of Simon & Schuster, Inc.

For information about special discounts for bulk purchases, please contact Simon & Schuster

Special Sales at 1-866-506-1949 or business@simonandschuster.com.

The Simon & Schuster Speakers Bureau can bring authors to your live event.

For more information or to book an event contact the Simon & Schuster

Speakers Bureau at 1-866-248-3049 or visit our website at www.simonspeakers.com.

Jacket designed by Dan Potash and Tom Daly

Interior designed by Karin Paprocki and Tom Daly

The illustrations for this book were rendered in marker and gouache.

The text of this book was set in Yana R & Yana B.

Manufactured in China 0815 SCP

2 4 6 8 10 9 7 5 3 1

Library of Congress Control Number 2015941993

ISBN 978-1-4814-5945-7 (hc)

ISBN 978-1-4814-5946-4 (eBook)

The genius, wit, and spirit of a nation
are discovered in its proverbs.

~FRANCIS BACON

PREFACE BY MARK R. LEVIN

It is such a joy watching my father, Jack, in action. He gets very excited about an idea for a book or painting, and the next thing you know, he is busy doing research at the local library or working at his artist's easel. In almost every case his books and latest artwork are intended for younger people and children. He tells me that, as it was for his parents and grandparents, it is very important for his generation to communicate with the next generation and future generations in ways that pass along wisdom, traditions, values, and, of course, patriotism.

In his earlier books—*Abraham Lincoln's Gettysburg Address Illustrated, George Washington: The Crossing,* and *Malice Toward None: Abraham Lincoln's Second Inaugural Address*—my father used seminal historical figures and events, with striking period illustrations, graphics, and photographs, to attract the attention of younger people and children and their interest in the lessons and the meaning of a good life and good citizenship. They are wonderful books. They are family books. And I find myself paging through them time and again.

Proverbs for Young People is my father's latest book. He developed all the scenes, drew all the figures, and applied his distinctive artistic method to tailoring the proverbs and relaying their timeless and universal messages to youngsters. While world events move at a rapid pace and technological change swirls around us, in a cheerful and novel style *Proverbs for Young People* teaches the importance of virtue and prudence and reminds us of certain truisms about good character, humanity, and life.

Proverbs for Young People is an absolutely delightful book. I doubt you can read it to your child or grandchild and show them the illustrations without putting a smile on both your faces. And no doubt it will lead to many hours of enjoyment and fascinating discussions.

INTRODUCTION

This little book of proverbs took me nearly sixty years to complete. I started working on it in 1959 and put it aside to finish another day. Because life is filled with events large and small that, by necessity, draw our attention, I actually forgot about the book. Now I am ninety years old. Not long ago, as I was going through some of my older work and projects, lo and behold, after all these years, I came across the early but incomplete version of the book.

I showed the book to my beloved wife, Norma. We've been married for sixty-five years. Many years ago, Norma taught fifth grade. Together, we started a private preschool and summer day camp. Norma has always loved being around young children and has been a wonderful mother to our three boys (now men). Norma loved the book and insisted that I finish it. And so I have. Thus, the short history behind this little book, *Proverbs for Young People.*

A proverb, according to the dictionary, is "a short traditional saying expressing a truth or moral instruction; an adage or old tale." In *Proverbs for Young People* I try to provide our young children—in my case, my grandchildren and great-grandchild—a basic understanding of good values. Unlike long or complicated lectures, proverbs teach moral and ethical principles and behavior in an understandable way to young children. I have added my artist's flair for colorful and fun drawings, which give the proverbs visual expression and make them even more relatable to young children.

I think of *Proverbs for Young People* as my little gift to our youngest generation, and the passing on of wise and useful advice from ancient times through life's continuum. I am very proud of this little book, and I hope you and your family enjoy it.

Jack E. Levin
Boynton Beach, Florida

Make every day

a cheerful day.

From little acorns,

large trees grow.

An apple a day

keeps the doctor away.

Kindness

brings kindness.

Your eyes should

not be larger than your stomach.

Only a game fish

swims upstream.

Children who play

with matches get burned.

Work ill done

must be done twice.

The doors of

wisdom are never closed.

You must crawl

before you can walk.

One robin

does not make a summer.

Early to bed

and early to rise

makes you  healthy,

wealthy,

and wise.

See no evil, hear no evil,

speak no evil.

Empty barrels

make the most noise.

Do unto others

as you would have others do unto you.

Don't count your

chickens before they're hatched.

Vessels large may venture more,

but little boats should keep near shore.

The early bird

catches the
worm.

A stitch in time

saves nine.

Prevention

is better than cure.

Little strokes

fell great oaks.

Practice

makes perfect.

Look before

you leap.

Never judge

a book by its cover.

Every tooth in your mouth

is more valuable than diamonds.

An empty bag

cannot stand alone.

If at first

you don't
succeed,

try,

try
again.

Love thy mother

and thy father.

All's well

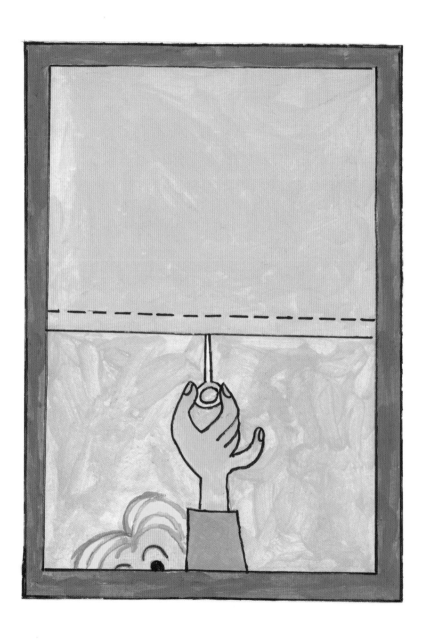

that ends well.

THE
END

Proverb Meanings

MAKE EVERY DAY A CHEERFUL DAY.
When you're cheerful and happy and make every moment count,
you also make people around you cheerful and happy.

FROM LITTLE ACORNS, LARGE TREES GROW.
From small beginnings, things of large size or importance can develop.

AN APPLE A DAY KEEPS THE DOCTOR AWAY.
Making healthy food choices is an important part of taking care of yourself.

KINDNESS BRINGS KINDNESS.
When you present yourself in a gentle, friendly way, you will find
people will respond to you in an agreeable manner.

YOUR EYES SHOULD NOT BE LARGER THAN YOUR STOMACH.
Don't try to do more than you are capable of doing.

ONLY A GAME FISH SWIMS UPSTREAM.
You're "game" if you are brave enough to take on very difficult challenges
and stick with them through all adversities until your final victory.

CHILDREN WHO PLAY WITH MATCHES GET BURNED.
If you participate in dangerous activities, you will probably suffer harm.

WORK ILL DONE MUST BE DONE TWICE.
Whether your work is physical or mental, if you do it poorly, don't care about it, or are
not interested in it, you'll have to do it over until it's right.

THE DOORS OF WISDOM ARE NEVER CLOSED.
There are always opportunities for you to learn, and it is up to you
to be aware of them. It's never too late to get an education.

YOU MUST CRAWL BEFORE YOU CAN WALK.
You must learn the basic steps before you can progress to more advanced tasks.

ONE ROBIN DOES NOT MAKE A SUMMER.
Just because something happens once doesn't mean it will happen again.

EARLY TO BED AND EARLY TO RISE MAKES YOU HEALTHY, WEALTHY, AND WISE.
When you have plenty of sleep and rest, you are alert when
opportunities arise and you can take advantage of them.

SEE NO EVIL, HEAR NO EVIL, SPEAK NO EVIL.
Don't be influenced by the bad behavior or mischief
of others, and don't spread gossip.

EMPTY BARRELS MAKE THE MOST NOISE.
People who speak loudly, complain endlessly, and have nothing to say
of importance talk the most and want to be noticed.

DO UNTO OTHERS AS YOU WOULD HAVE OTHERS DO UNTO YOU.
Act friendly, cheerfully, kindly, and thoughtfully toward people and
animals and you will be treated the same in return.

DON'T COUNT YOUR CHICKENS BEFORE THEY'RE HATCHED.
Do not take for granted that you will succeed until you do.

VESSELS LARGE MAY VENTURE MORE, BUT LITTLE BOATS SHOULD KEEP NEAR SHORE.
If you are confident that you know enough to try a new or challenging task,
take the chance. But if you aren't as sure of yourself or your skills,
take small steps before larger ones.

THE EARLY BIRD CATCHES THE WORM.
If you start something early, you have a better chance at succeeding.

A STITCH IN TIME SAVES NINE.
Prompt attention to a minor problem will avoid major problems later.

PREVENTION IS BETTER THAN CURE.
It is better to prevent something undesirable from
happening than to have to fix it later.

LITTLE STROKES FELL GREAT OAKS.

Great things can be achieved in small stages, and with persistent
effort you will eventually see results.

PRACTICE MAKES PERFECT.

Work over and over again at what you are trying to achieve,
and you will become better at it. Stick to it!

LOOK BEFORE YOU LEAP.

Think carefully before you act.

NEVER JUDGE A BOOK BY ITS COVER.

Don't form an opinion about something or someone
based on outward appearance.

EVERY TOOTH IN YOUR MOUTH IS MORE VALUABLE THAN DIAMONDS.

Take good care of your teeth. Brush them every day. Dentists can never replace
original teeth; they can only replace them with false teeth.

AN EMPTY BAG CANNOT STAND ALONE.

Without love, knowledge, inspiration, and hard work,
you cannot function on your own.

IF AT FIRST YOU DON'T SUCCEED, TRY, TRY AGAIN.

If you keep trying with fortitude and determination,
success will ultimately be yours.

LOVE THY MOTHER AND THY FATHER.

You will never have closer or dearer friends to you in the world than your parents.
Love and cherish them while they are available to you.

ALL'S WELL THAT ENDS WELL.

If you are happy with a project at the end, then it was worth
the difficulty or challenges along the way.